BUILDING BLOCKS OF COMPUTER SCIENCE

LOGIC in CODING

Written by Echo Elise González

Illustrated by Graham Ross

a Scott Fetzer company
Chicago

World Book, Inc.
180 North LaSalle Street
Suite 900
Chicago, Illinois 60601
USA

For information about other World Book publications, visit our website at **www.worldbook.com** or call **1-800-WORLDBK (967-5325)**.
For information about sales to schools and libraries, call 1-800-975-3250 (United States), or 1-800-837-5365 (Canada).

Library of Congress Cataloging-in-Publication Data for this volume has been applied for.

Building Blocks of Computer Science
ISBN: 978-0-7166-2883-5 (set, hc.)

Logic in Coding
ISBN: 978-0-7166-2887-3 (hc.)

Also available as:
ISBN: 978-0-7166-2895-8 (e-book)

1st printing August 2020

Acknowledgments:
Art by Graham Ross/The Bright Agency
Series reviewed by Peter Jang/Actualize Coding Bootcamp

TABLE OF CONTENTS

There is a glossary on page 30. Terms defined in the glossary are in type **that looks like this** on their first appearance.

LOGIC!
How do you do?
We're the **logic gates.**
AND
OR
We are basic parts of the electronic **circuits** inside a computer.
We can receive **input** information in the form of electrical signals...
AND
INPUT
...And we can produce an **output.**
OUTPUT
AND
OR

We make decisions for the computer!
AND
OR

LOGIC
We use **logic** to determine what kind of output to give.

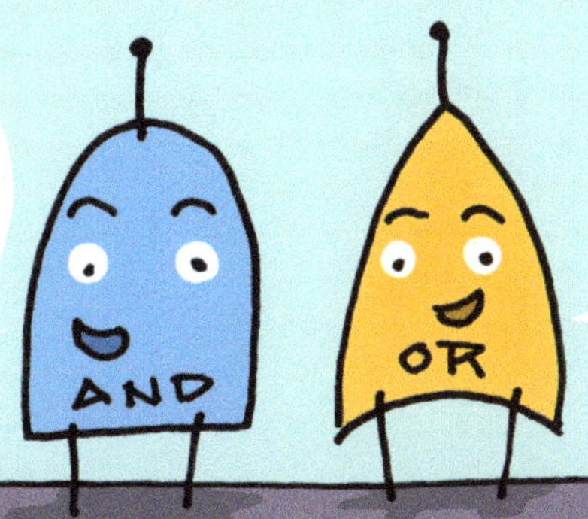
My name is "AND." My logic is based on the AND rule.
To get a positive output, BOTH my inputs have to be positive.
And I'm "OR." My logic is based on the OR rule.
To get a positive output, AT LEAST ONE of my inputs has to be positive.
AND
OR

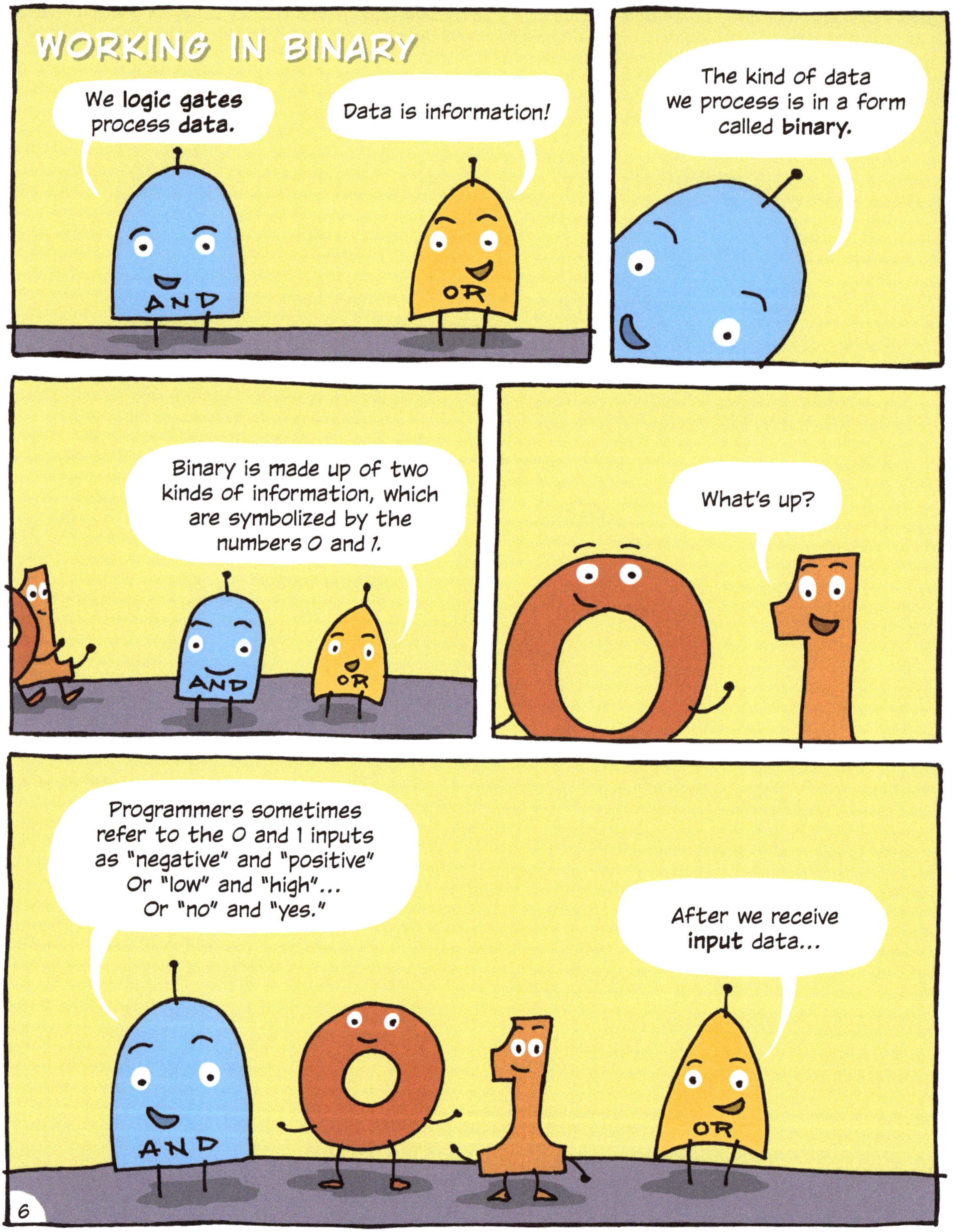

WORKING IN BINARY

Programmers sometimes refer to the 0 and 1 inputs as "negative" and "positive" Or "low" and "high"... Or "no" and "yes."

After we receive **input** data...

AND

OR

We use our logic to process it...
AND
OR

And we produce an **output**!
AND
OR

The output is also in the form of an electrical signal.
0
1

This signal tells a **transistor** whether to switch on or off.

An output of 0 means the switch turns OFF.
OFF
AND

ON
An output of 1 means the switch turns ON.
AND

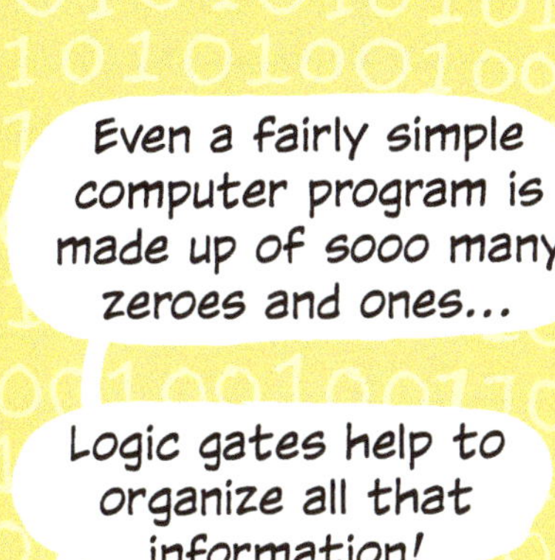
Even a fairly simple computer program is made up of sooo many zeroes and ones...
Logic gates help to organize all that information!

OR
AND

TRUE OR FALSE?

The **logic** that we use to process **data** can be written out in mathematical tables.

These are called **truth tables.**

A truth table shows all the possible combinations of **inputs** and the correct **output** for each combination.

Here's my truth table.

My inputs can be any of the possible combinations of 0 and 1. Those are on the left side of the table.

On the right side are the correct outputs for each of the input combinations.

A *1* signal represents an electric charge, and a *0* represents no electric charge.

AND truth table

	INPUT 1		INPUT 2		OUTPUT
IF	0	AND	0	THEN	0
IF	0	AND	1	THEN	0
IF	1	AND	0	THEN	0
IF	1	AND	1	THEN	1

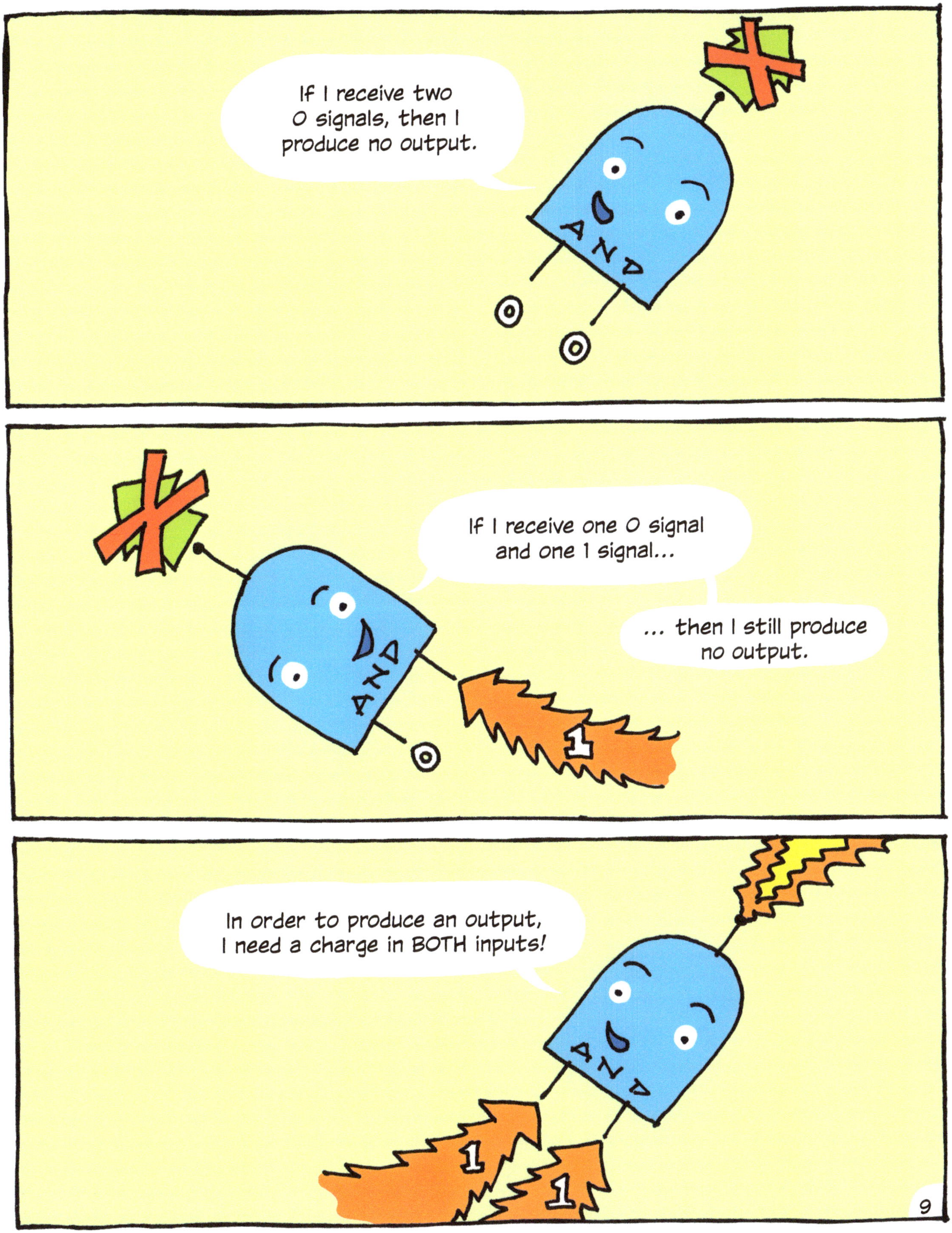

If I receive two
0 signals, then I
produce no output.

My **input** combinations are the same as those in AND's truth table.

But, some of my **outputs** are different.

They're different because I'm using OR **logic** to produce my outputs.

OR truth table

	INPUT 1		INPUT 2		OUTPUT
IF	0	AND	0	THEN	0
IF	0	AND	1	THEN	1
IF	1	AND	0	THEN	1
IF	1	AND	1	THEN	1

OR

If I receive two 0 signals, then I produce no output.
OR
0
0

If I receive one 0 signal and one 1 signal...
...then I do produce an output!
OR
0
1

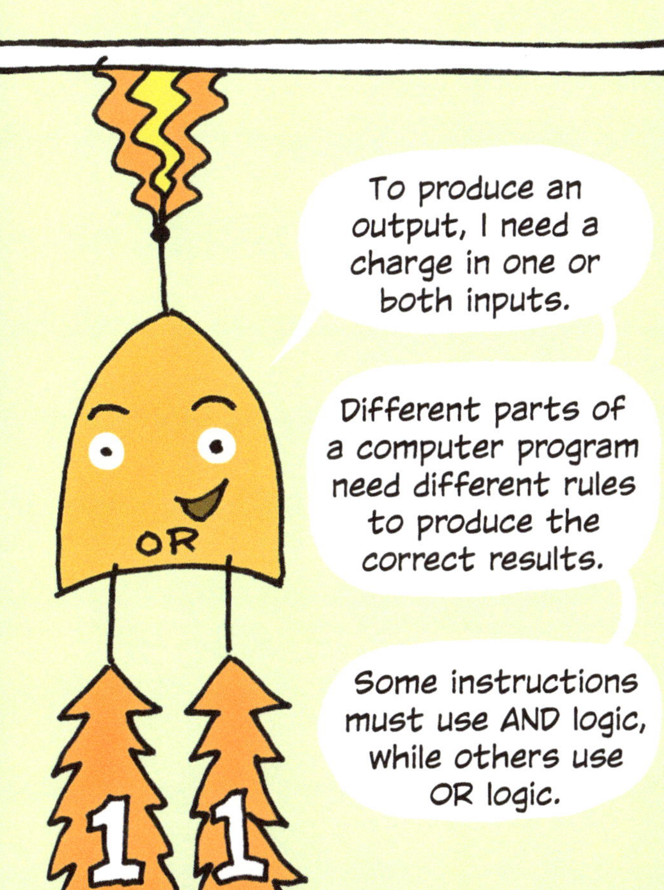
To produce an output, I need a charge in one or both inputs.
Different parts of a computer program need different rules to produce the correct results.
Some instructions must use AND logic, while others use OR logic.
OR
1
1

There are other kinds of **logic gates**, too!
NOT
NAND
OR
XOR

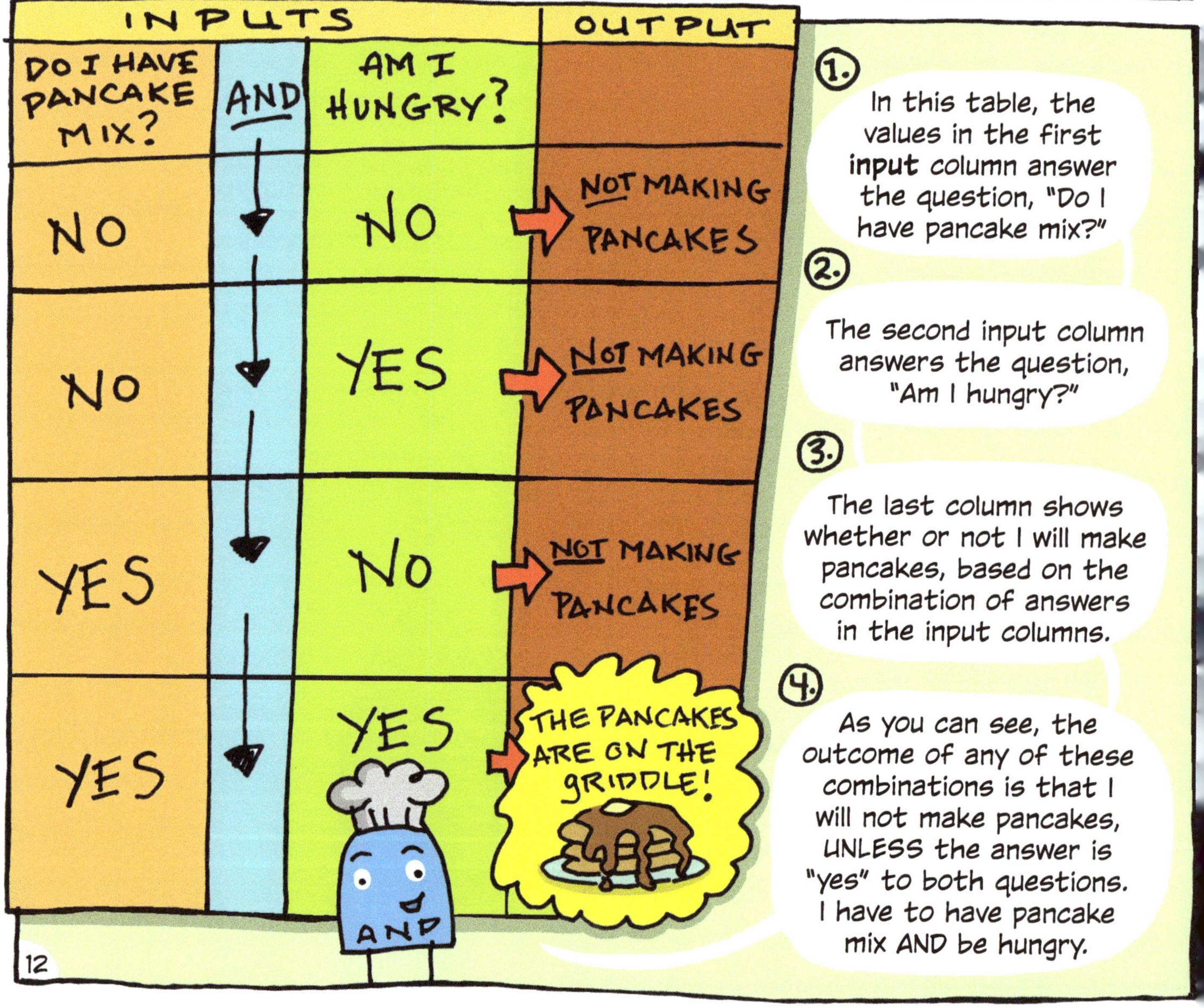

INPUTS			OUTPUT
DO I HAVE PANCAKE MIX?	AND	AM I HUNGRY?	
NO	↓	NO	NOT MAKING PANCAKES
NO	↓	YES	NOT MAKING PANCAKES
YES	↓	NO	NOT MAKING PANCAKES
YES	↓	YES	THE PANCAKES ARE ON THE GRIDDLE!

AND

1. In this table, the values in the first **input** column answer the question, "Do I have pancake mix?"

2. The second input column answers the question, "Am I hungry?"

3. The last column shows whether or not I will make pancakes, based on the combination of answers in the input columns.

4. As you can see, the outcome of any of these combinations is that I will not make pancakes, UNLESS the answer is "yes" to both questions. I have to have pancake mix AND be hungry.

I have a bowl of peas, but I need a spoon or a fork to eat them.
Let's use an OR logic truth table to figure out if I can eat the peas!
OR
1.
Here, the values in the first column answer the question, "Do I have a fork?"
2.
The values in the second column answer the question, "Do I have a spoon?"
3.
The output for each combination is shown in the last column.
4.
As you can see, I can eat the peas if at least one of the input answers is YES. I have to have a fork OR a spoon.
INPUTS
OUTPUT
DO I HAVE A FORK?
OR =
DO I HAVE A SPOON?
NO
NO
CANNOT EAT THE PEAS
NO
YES
CAN EAT THE PEAS
YES
NO
CAN EAT THE PEAS
YES
YES
CAN EAT THE PEAS
OR

STATEMENTS
So, how do programmers actually use this **logic** in coding?
Much of computer programming involves writing **statements.**
AND
OR
A statement is a command or instruction for the computer.
PUT TWO SLICES OF BREAD ON THE PLATE
PUT THE SLICES OF BREAD ON A PLATE
PUT PEANUT BUTTER ON ONE OF THE SLICES
PUT JELLY ON THE OTHER SIDE
PUT THE SLICES TOGETHER
A set of statements that works together to accomplish a specific goal is called a **function.**

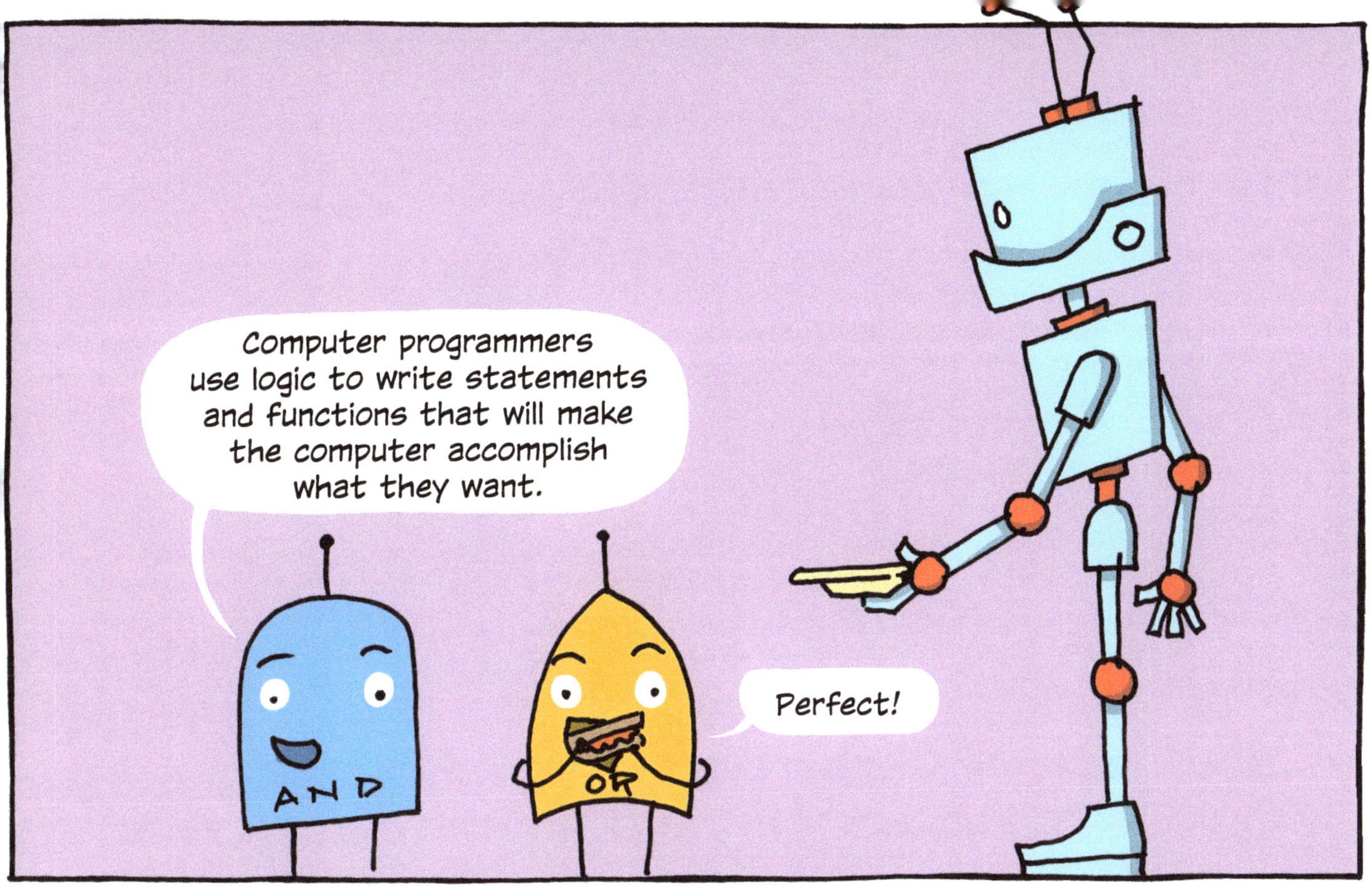

Computer programmers use logic to write statements and functions that will make the computer accomplish what they want.

Perfect!

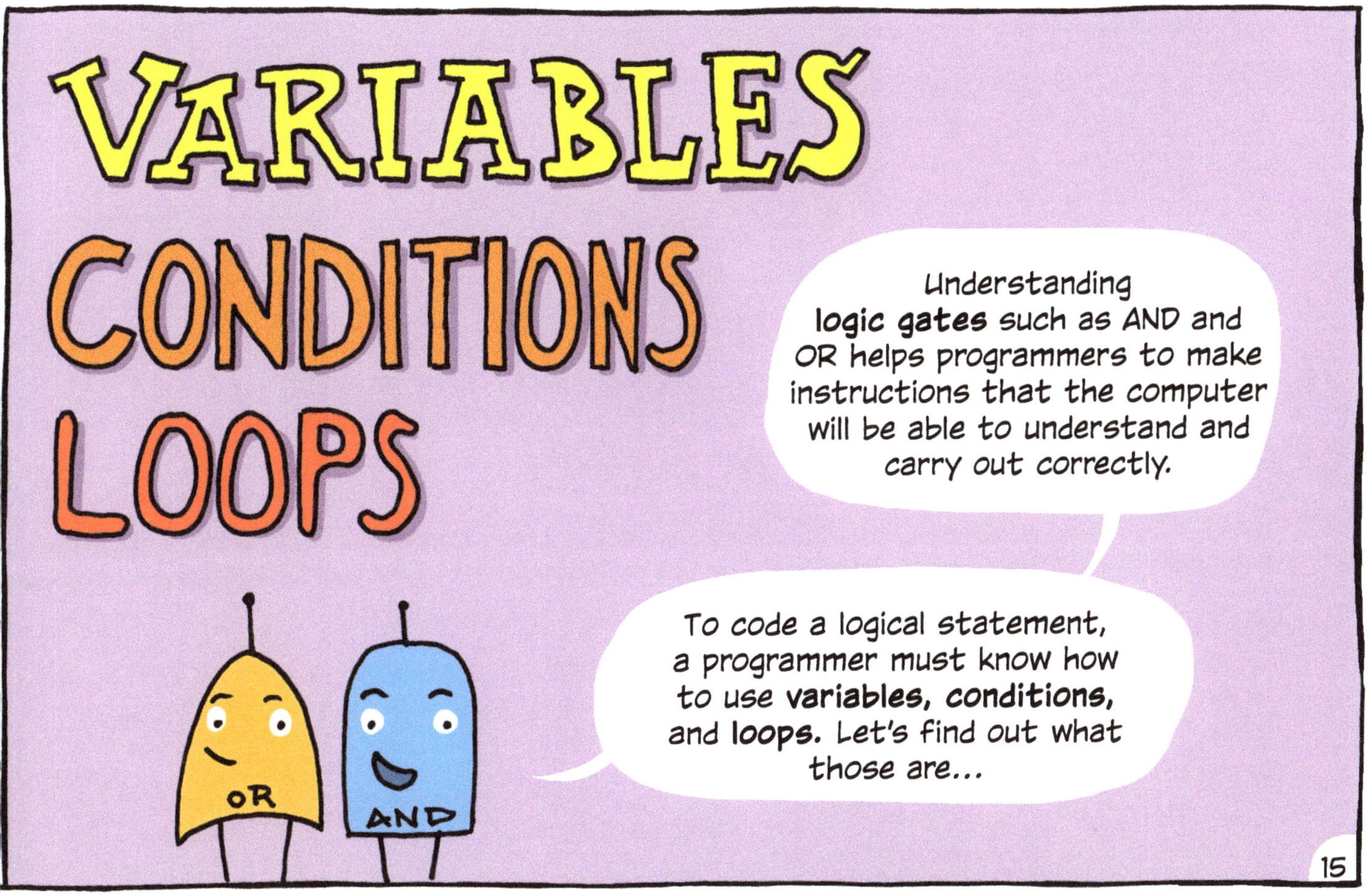

VARIABLES CONDITIONS LOOPS

Understanding **logic gates** such as AND and OR helps programmers to make instructions that the computer will be able to understand and carry out correctly.

To code a logical statement, a programmer must know how to use **variables, conditions,** and **loops.** Let's find out what those are...

VARIABLES
I'm programming a video game.
In my game, I want my character to be able to walk left or right.
AND
VARIABLE
when right arrow key pressed
move 1 step right
I'll use a **variable** to control my character's movement.
A variable is a piece of information that can vary. It can be changed.
AND

This variable moves the character based on which button the player presses.
So, now, when the player presses the right arrow button on their keyboard, the character will move 1 step to the right.
AND
When the computer receives instructions from this variable, **logic gates** will help it decide the correct **output.**
AND
In this case, it will use the **logic** that IF the right arrow key is pressed, THEN the character will move 1 step to the right.
when left arrow Key pressed
move 1 step left
When the player presses the left arrow button, the character will move 1 step to the left.

CONDITIONS

I'd like my character to be able to move faster, too.

To do this, I can set up a **condition.**

A condition tells the computer to run a code only under a particular circumstance.

AND

My condition will tell the computer to use **logic** to determine whether the character should be moving quickly or slowly.

when
if key space pressed? then
move 20 steps
else
move 5 steps

AND

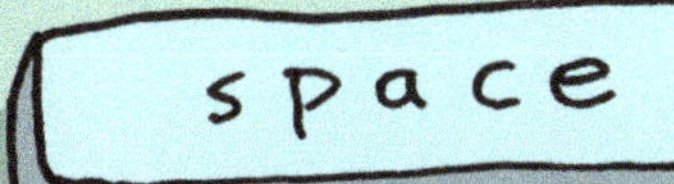

My condition states that IF the player presses the spacebar while they are pressing an arrow key,...

...THEN the character will move 10 steps.

move 1 step

Or ELSE, if the player only presses the arrow key without pressing the spacebar, the character will only move 1 step.

The player controls the hero with the arrow keys and the space bar.

But I'll let the computer control the dragon.

SPACE

I want the computer to move the dragon to random positions around the screen.

This pattern will require the computer to perform the same task over and over again...

...which means I should use a **loop** to create this instruction.

A loop is a piece of code that causes a part of the program to run over and over again.

I'll need to add a loop that runs forever, so that the action will continue repeating throughout the game.

My loop asks the computer to place the dragon in a new random position every 1 second.

I want my character to change color whenever she touches the dragon.

She should turn red to alert the player that she's touching the dragon.

This will require both a **condition** AND a **loop**.

CONDITION

LOOP

if touching Dragon ▽ ? then

set color ▽ effects to red ▽

else

set color ▽ effects to blue ▽

So, I'll create a condition that asks the computer to change the character's color to red only when she is touching the dragon.

And, since we want this to happen not just once but every time she touches the dragon, I will also use a loop.
Combining a condition and a loop is useful in situations in which you want a computer to check over and over again if a certain condition is true.
forever
if touching ? then
set color effects to red
else
set color effects to blue
AND
TAP
TAP
TAP

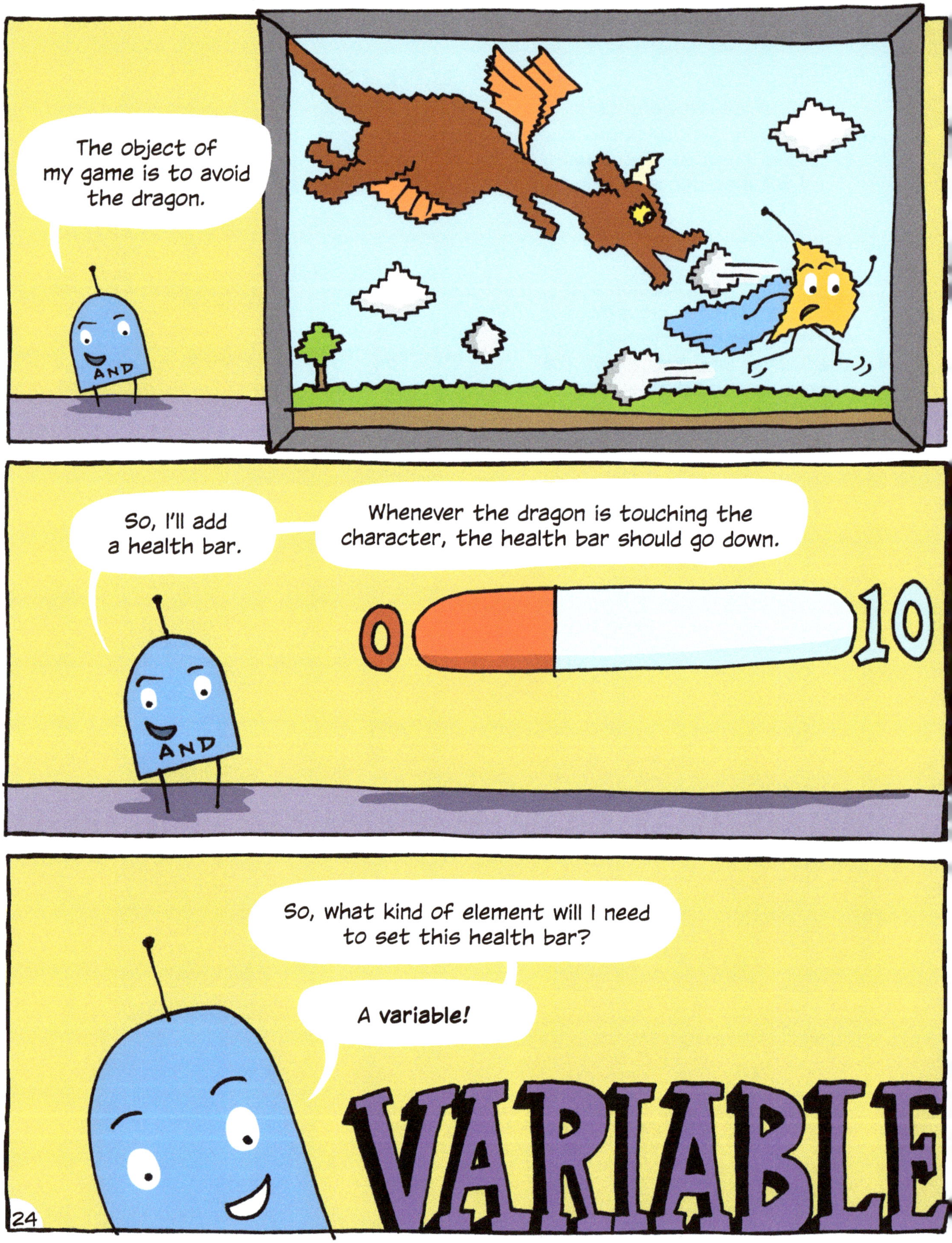

The object of my game is to avoid the dragon.

AND

forever
if touching dragon then
set colors effects to red
change health by -1
else
set color effects to blue

The health bar will change throughout the program.

This variable will allow me to include this changing piece of information in the program.

0 10

I will add the variable to the **condition** that I just created.

Now, whenever the dragon is touching the character, the character will turn red AND...

AND

...her health bar will go down.

0 10

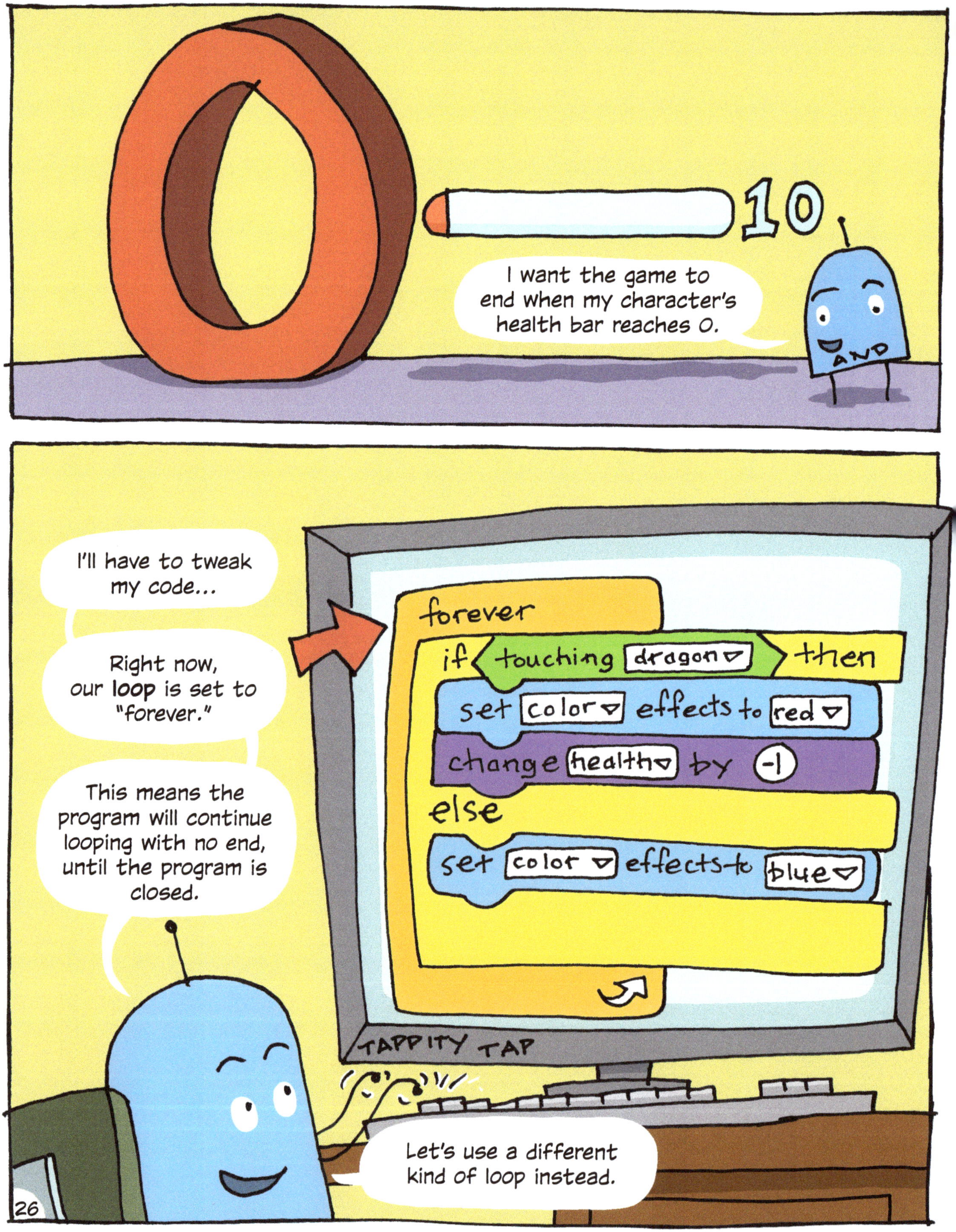

I'll have to tweak my code...

Right now, our **loop** is set to "forever."

This means the program will continue looping with no end, until the program is closed.

forever
if touching dragon then
set color effects to red
change health by -1
else
set color effects to blue

TAPPITY TAP

Let's use a different kind of loop instead.

repeat until health ≠ 0
if touching dragon then
set color effects to red
change health by -1
else
set color effects to blue
0
10
TAP TAP
AND
Now our loop will only continue repeating until the health bar reaches 0.

Writing a computer program like a game means making a lot of careful decisions.

With the help of **logic**, we can make all the right decisions to produce the program we want.

TAP TAP

OR

AND

Without logic, computer programs wouldn't make any sense.

POOF

In fact, they wouldn't exist at all!

Throw the ball to AND
OR
Understanding the basic elements of code, like **variables, conditions,** and **loops,** enables us to communicate logically and clearly with the computer.
AND
Pick up, THEN throw.
It's also important to understand how computers use logic to make decisions.
With this knowledge, we can create effective programs that ask the computer to do exactly what we want them to!
So, when you find yourself making your own program...
AND
Remember: It's always helpful to think logically!
AND
OR

GLOSSARY

binary a numbering system that uses two digits—*0* and *1*.

circuit a loop that an electric current can follow.

computer chip a tiny piece of the material silicon that holds an electronic circuit.

condition a statement that can be true or false. A program may tell a computer to run a piece of code if a certain condition is true.

data information that a computer processes or stores.

function a set of statements that works together to accomplish a specific goal.

logic the rules of proper reasoning.

logic gate a circuit that can receive two electric inputs and produce one electric output. The output is determined by the logic of the circuit.

loop a piece of code that causes part of a program to run over and over again.

statement a command or instruction for the computer.

transistor a tiny device that controls the flow of electric current in a computer chip.

truth table a table that shows the output for different combinations of inputs, based on logic.

variable a value, or piece of information, that can change.

GO ONLINE

Building Blocks of Computer Science
ACTIVITIES BOOKS
Activities
Practice your programming skills and test your knowledge with these games and projects based on the *Building Blocks of Computer Science* series.
Robot friend
Can you program a robot? In this game, you
Algorithm origami
Can you follow the steps to make an origami
Are you ready to test your logic skills? Go to this website to find the Make a Truth Table activity and all kinds of other fun games and activities.
www.worldbook.com /BuildingBlocks
AND
OR

INDEX

www.ingramcontent.com/pod-product-compliance
Ingram Content Group UK Ltd.
Pitfield, Milton Keynes, MK11 3LW, UK
UKHW061958290726
14090UKWH00021B/1267